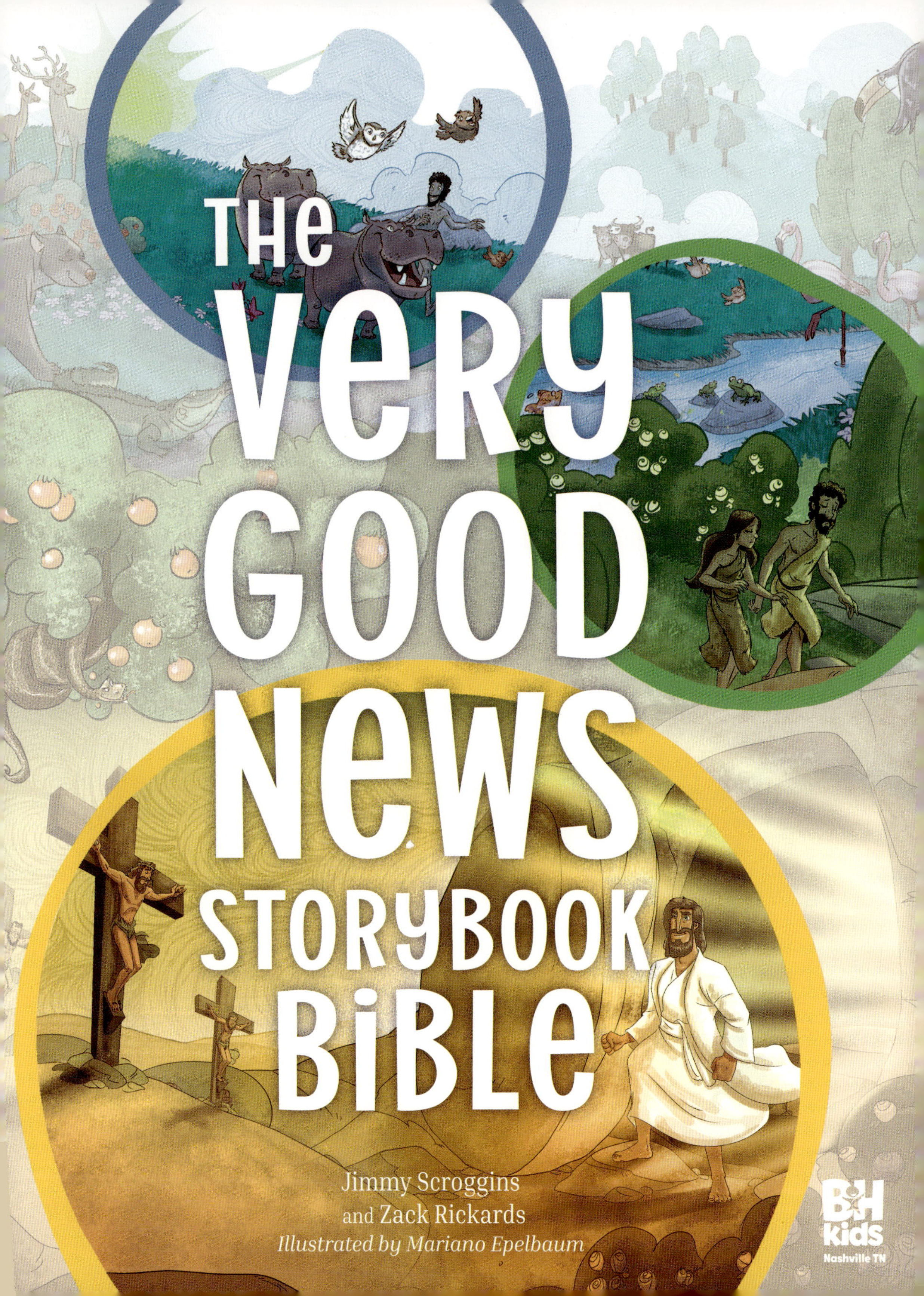

The Very Good News Storybook Bible

Jimmy Scroggins
and Zack Rickards
Illustrated by Mariano Epelbaum

B&H Kids
Nashville TN

FROM JiMMY—

To my wife, Kristin. Your grace, elegance, and wisdom never cease to amaze me. Your husband, your children, and your grandchildren all rise up and call you blessed.

And to our grandchildren—James, Wyatt, Willow Kate, and Haven Hope (plus all the others yet to be born). All of you are wanted and loved so much. May you learn to love Jesus with all of your hearts.

FROM ZaCK—

To my mom and dad. Thank you for always pointing me to Jesus.

To my wife, Amber. There's no one else I'd rather do life with and share laughs with than you. Thank you for your constant encouragement and unwavering support as we point our three blessings to Jesus.

And finally, to my kids. Ruthie, Crusen, and Corbett. Daddy loves you, but more importantly, God loves you more! That's the very good news.

Published in 2025 by B&H Publishing Group,
Brentwood, Tennessee.

ISBN: 978-1-0877-2969-5

Dewey Decimal Classification: J220.95
SUBHD: BIBLE—STORIES / GOSPEL / CONVERSION
Printed in Shenzhen, Guangdong, China, December 2024
1 2 3 4 5 6 • 29 28 27 26 25

INTRODUCTiON

Did you know the Bible is one *big* story about the one true God? It is made up of hundreds of stories about hundreds of people and God's love for them. There's a big word for this: *metanarrative*, which basically means a bunch of little stories that make up one *big* story. The big story? That's God's big Plan!

The coolest fact about Bible stories is that they are true! These little stories all have a pattern that matches the same pattern in the BIG story. The Bible tells the story about God's Plan for the way things should be. The Bible also tells the story of the Fall, which is how sin entered the world. Sin breaks God's design and leads people into brokenness. But that's not the whole story. The Bible also tells us about the only way to fix the brokenness—the gospel. It tells us how to get back to God's Plan again! This pattern shows up over and over in the stories of the Bible. One way to explain this pattern is a tool called the 3 Circles. The picture below is what it looks like.

This pattern is in the little stories and the big story. It all starts with God's Plan. **IN THE PLAN, EVERYTHING IS PERFECT.** Brothers and sisters don't argue. Parents love each other forever. Grandparents don't die. There are no wars or fighting anywhere in the world. Everyone gets along and is happy. This sounds awesome, right? It is! But something goes wrong. It's called sin.

Sin is anything we do that is not in God's Plan. We make a choice we think is better than what God says is best. Everyone sins. You sin. **AND WHEN WE SIN, WE LEAVE GOD'S PLAN AND END UP IN BROKENNESS (THE FALL).**

Brokenness is no fun and makes you feel bad inside. But brokenness isn't the main problem. The main problem is sin. Sin is a huge problem because when we sin, we break God's law. When people break the law in our town, the judge at the courthouse declares them guilty. And then the judge makes them pay a penalty, maybe a fine or time in jail. God is a loving Father, but He is also a righteous judge. When we break God's law, He declares us guilty and will make us pay a penalty like death and separation from God forever. Like we said, sin is a huge problem.

Well, nobody likes living in brokenness, so we all try to fix it. Sometimes we try to get out of brokenness with good things, like friends and family. Other times we try to get out of brokenness with bad things, like lying or hiding. Brokenness feels bad. But God uses brokenness for our good. When we feel brokenness in our lives, it makes us want to change. Brokenness helps us see our sins and makes us want to get back to God's Plan.

Sadly, no matter how hard we try, we can't fix our own brokenness, and we can't forgive our own sins. Don't worry, though; there is good news! God loves us, and He created a way for us to get out of brokenness. God made a way that our sins can be forgiven forever—the gospel. **THE GOSPEL IS THE VERY GOOD NEWS THAT JESUS CAME TO EARTH AND LIVED A PERFECT LIFE.** Jesus never sinned, not even once. He died on the cross for the sins of everyone who believes in Him, and He paid the penalty to the judge for us. Then God raised Jesus from the dead.

We can get out of brokenness when we repent and believe the gospel. *Repent* is a Bible word that means to turn around. *Believe* means to rely on Jesus as the one way to escape brokenness. When we repent of our sins and believe in Jesus, God forgives our sins. God welcomes us into His family, accepts us, and loves us forever. Once we repent and believe, we can start to recover (get back) and pursue (chase after) God's Plan again!

This is the BIG story of the Bible, and you can see this pattern repeated in all the little stories that make up the Bible, including the stories in this book you're holding! Once you learn to see this pattern in the Bible, you can use the 3 Circles to talk to your friends about God's Very Good News!

CONTENTS

1

The First Story Ever

Genesis 1–3

The best place to start is the beginning! In the beginning there was nothing. Well, nothing but God the Father, God the Son, and God the Holy Spirit. Since there was nothing but Him in the beginning, we know that God created everything. **God had an awesome plan for the world.** He planned the light and the darkness and called them day and night. He separated the waters, creating heaven and earth. He gathered the water together and allowed the land to appear. It was all planned very carefully and with a specific purpose.

The Plan

Next God planned every plant, from the giant sequoia tree down to the tiniest grain of rice. He designed all the beautiful, sweet-smelling flowers and the delicious fruit trees. Even the vegetables like brussels sprouts and lima beans were part of His Plan. He didn't just design the earth, He planned the sun, moon, stars, and planets in outer space too.

God planned and designed and created every sea creature in the oceans deep, from the octopus with its eight legs to the seahorse with its curly tail. He created every bird in the sky, from the soaring falcon to the zipping hummingbird. And He went on to plan every animal, those that growl, roar, squeak, hiss, and bark. He created all the bugs you've ever seen plus the ones you've never seen. And then, after all this work, God planned His most wonderful and special creation: people! God made people in His own image, to look, act, and love like Him. The first person God created was a man He called *Adam*.

Adam lived in the beautiful garden called Eden, and he and God walked together and talked together. Everything was exactly the way God had planned it to be. And God made sure Adam had plenty to eat. Oranges. Apples. Nuts. Berries. Bananas. Potatoes. Carrots. Mangoes. Adam was allowed to eat anything from any tree or plant in the garden. Except for one tree. Adam was not allowed to eat from the tree of the knowledge of good and evil. God gave Adam this one command to make sure everything stayed good—the way God had planned it.

God also planned for Adam to work. His job was to name every single animal, and he couldn't just call them all "monkey." Adam noticed every animal had a partner. There were boys and girls—males and females—of every kind. But Adam didn't have a female partner. So God put him into a deep sleep and, while Adam was sleeping, took out one of his ribs. From Adam's rib God designed and created a woman. The woman would be Adam's perfect partner. Adam gave her the name *Eve*. God made Adam and Eve to be married to each other, to love each other and take care of one another. They were partners in taking care of God's beautiful garden. God wanted them to have children, who would have children, who would have children, so that the earth would be filled with people. Everything was just as God planned it to be.

But one day the tricky serpent, who was Satan, spoke to Eve. He told her God was hiding something . . . that if she and Adam ate the fruit from the tree of the knowledge of good and evil, they could be as wise as God. Eve might have thought that if she and Adam ate the fruit, maybe they could be wise "planet planners" like God! And the fruit probably did look tasty. So Eve bit into the fruit and then gave it to Adam, who ate some too.

At this moment, something terrible had happened. **ADAM AND EVE HAD SINNED. THEY HAD DEPARTED FROM GOD'S PERFECT PLAN.**

THE FALL

Suddenly, they realized they were naked and tried to cover themselves. They felt scared. Those scary feelings Adam and Eve had? That was them feeling brokenness for the first time. This very first sin is called "the Fall." We call it the Fall because it's like Adam and Eve fell down from God's Plan and hurt themselves. God knew what Adam and Eve had done, and He already had a way to forgive their sin and fix their hurt and brokenness. One day God would send Jesus, and Jesus would make everything good again. But for now, Adam and Eve were in trouble.

Like a loving Father, God came to find Adam and Eve. They were naked. They were scared. That brokenness made them feel *bad*. They heard God coming, but instead of walking with Him in the light of the beautiful garden, they hid. When God called out and asked if they had eaten the one fruit He had told them not to eat, Adam immediately blamed Eve. Then Eve immediately blamed the serpent.

God cursed the serpent because Satan was trying to mess up God's Plan. God told the serpent that a man—a descendant of Adam and Eve—would one day come and crush his head. He told Adam and Eve that their lives would be hard. He sent them out of the garden of Eden forever. They had to start over.

But God still loved Adam and Eve, and He didn't give up on them. God made clothes for them out of animal skins and helped them start their new life outside of the garden. God knew this would not be the last time His Plan would be broken because of sin. Adam and Eve had tried to fix the brokenness in their own way. But their way didn't work. They tried to hide and

cover themselves. They tried blaming someone else. But they couldn't fix the brokenness, and they couldn't forgive their own sin. Only God, the Planet Planner, could do that. And He would! One day God would send His Son, Jesus, to crush the serpent's head. **JESUS WOULD FIX THE BROKENNESS IN THE WORLD ONCE AND FOR ALL.** And *that* is God's amazing good news.

THE VERY GOOD NEWS

Generation after generation of Adam and Eve's descendants looked forward to that day when Jesus would come. But until then, God would keep providing chances for His people to recover and pursue His Plan. People would keep sinning. But they would keep repenting. They would keep recovering. God's Plan is really big. The Fall was really bad. But the good news is really, really good.

2

A ZOO ON A BOAT

GENESIS 6–9

After Adam and Eve got kicked out of the garden, things were bad—*really* bad. They did have kids who had kids who had kids. The earth was filled with people, but that's not the bad part. The bad part was that everything the people thought, imagined, and did was totally evil. People had forgotten God's awesome Plan for the world. And all those evil thoughts and actions created all kinds of brokenness.

God was very sad about the brokenness in the world and sorry He had ever made people. He decided to wash the earth clean, using water to wipe every living thing—person, animal, bird—off the face of the earth. But

THE PLAN

ONE MAN LOVED GOD AND WANTED TO FOLLOW HIS AWESOME PLAN: Noah. When God looked at Noah, Noah's faith moved the heart of God.

God spoke to Noah and told him about His decision to wash the earth clean with a flood. The flood would cover the entire world and destroy everything, including all the animals and all the people. The flood was going to be the end of all the sinning, evil, and brokenness in the world.

The flood sounded like bad news to Noah, but the good news was that God would use Noah and his family to start over. And God had a very important job for Noah. He was to build a boat. Well, not really a boat, but an ark. Noah had never seen an ark, so God's Plan must have sounded crazy at first. God wanted to save Noah's family; they just needed to trust God and build the ark.

Noah was a farmer, not a boat builder. Plus, he didn't live near any water, so he had never needed a boat before. But he trusted God. God gave Noah instructions to build an ark big enough to hold Noah's family, at least two of every kind of animal, and all their food. The ark would be huge, but it would still float!

Noah was more than five hundred years old when he started building. The people around him might have wondered what he was doing. **THEY DID NOT UNDERSTAND THEIR SIN AND BROKENNESS.** They continued to do whatever they wanted, hiding from the pain they felt and the pain they caused. Little did they know that God was providing a way out for Noah and his family—a fresh start to recover and pursue God's original, awesome Plan.

THE FALL

Day after day Noah worked. He stayed faithful to God and continued to build the ark . . . for nearly one hundred years! Finally the ark was finished, and it was time for the flood. God brought at least two of every animal, bird, and creeping creature to Noah, and the ark-boarding began! When Noah, his wife, their three sons, their wives, all the animals, and all the food was in the ark, God shut the door.

Then it happened. *Drip. Drip drop.* Noah and his family could hear the raindrops hitting the roof. The drops quickly turned into a storm of rain pounding on the ark. It rained and rained and rained. Then they felt it. The ark broke free from the ground and began to float. It rained for forty days and forty nights with no breaks. But then one day the rain stopped. The ark was floating alone on a world that was completely covered with water. It floated for a very, very long time.

While they floated, Noah and his family must have thought about what had happened outside the ark. Every bug and animal not on the ark? Dead. All the birds who had nowhere to land? Dead. And saddest of all, the people were dead too. They were punished for their sins. God provided a way out for Noah and his family because they believed God and got on the ark.

After many months in the ark, Noah sent out a dove to see if the waters had dried up. The dove went and came back. After a few tries, the dove didn't return. She had found dry ground! Then one day Noah looked out to see land! God told Noah and his family to get off the ark. They released the animals to fill the earth once again and return to the way God had planned for life to be in the beginning.

Noah built an altar and worshiped the Lord. God promised never to flood the entire earth or curse the ground again. To remind His people of this promise, God placed a beautiful rainbow in the sky. Every time God's people saw the rainbow, they would remember God's promise to them. God told Noah and his family the same thing He had told Adam and Eve—have children and fill the world with people.

This was all good news. But God knew it wasn't the final solution. Noah and his family would sin. People would hurt and kill each other again. People would forget about God's awesome Plan for them.

NOAH'S FAMILY GOT A NEW START, A CHANCE TO RECOVER AND PURSUE GOD'S PLAN, but there was still a promise to be fulfilled. There was still a Son who would one day come.

THE VERY GOOD NEWS

When God rescued Noah and his family, He gave us a picture of how He would one day rescue all kinds of people by sending His Son. Just like Noah and his family were rescued from the flood, God would rescue people from their sins by sending Jesus. And that's the Very Good News!

3

THE REALLY BIG PROMISE

GENESIS 12–18

Many years had gone by since Noah and his family left the ark, and the world was filled with people again. God was ready to set His Plan into motion to deliver mankind from the brokenness of their sin. His Plan was to start with one man, Abram. Now this choice was already a little odd because Abram wasn't exactly young. In fact, he was seventy-five years old! God told Abram that all people for all time would be blessed because of him and his family. This was also strange because Abram and his wife had never been able to have children.

First, God asked Abram to move to a new land. So Abram gathered his family and everything he owned and moved where God told him to go—a place called Canaan. There God gave Abram some really good news: Abram would have a son! God showed Abram a night sky full of twinkling stars and said Abram would have so many kids, grandkids, great-grandkids, great-great-grandkids, and so on that no one could count them, just like the stars in the sky! God changed Abram's name to *Abraham,* which means "dad of nations," because God was going to make Abraham the father of so many people. **THE PLAN** **THROUGH ABRAHAM, GOD WAS GOING TO ALLOW THE WORLD'S PEOPLE TO TRULY RECOVER AND TO PURSUE HIS PLAN FOR THEIR LIVES.** What Abraham didn't know was that one of his great-great-great-great-great-grandkids would be Jesus. Abraham was part of God's awesome Plan. So when God promised him a son? *That* was good news!

THE FALL

Years and years passed, and still no son for Abraham. **HE AND HIS WIFE, SARAH, WERE GETTING NERVOUS AND THOUGHT THEY NEEDED TO FIX THIS PROBLEM ON THEIR OWN INSTEAD OF WAITING ON GOD.** They decided Abraham should have a child with one of Sarah's servants, but it did not turn out the way they had hoped. In fact, things got worse. A lot of people got hurt. Ever since the Fall in the garden, people had a hard time following God's Plan.

Abraham wanted to recover and pursue God's Plan. So, Abraham waited for God to do what He had said He would do. Abraham waited to be a blessing

to the world as God had promised. It felt like time was running out. Then when Abraham was ninety-nine years old, God spoke to him again. He promised Abraham that he and Sarah would still have a son. Abraham . . . laughed.

Abraham explained that he was really old—like, great-grandpa old—and Sarah was really old—like, great-grandma old! How could they have a baby at *their* age? But God said it again: They would have a baby boy within one year. When Sarah heard all of this, she laughed. Because of their laughter, God told them to name their son *Isaac*, which means "laughter."

As the days passed, Sarah's belly grew bigger and bigger. Then the day came when her baby boy arrived. Sarah laughed to herself. She said that others would laugh when she told them the story of how God allowed a great-grandpa-aged man and a great-grandma-aged woman to have a baby. **They named their baby *Isaac*, and laughter filled their home. God had kept His promise to them.** But there was a really big promise still waiting.

The Very Good News

Sin had entered the world through one man, Adam, and corrupted it. But God already had a Plan to fix it. He chose to start His special family who would fulfill His promise with one man, Abraham. Isaac was the first baby born in this special family with a promise, but he wouldn't be the last . . . or the most important. God's promise to bless the world and fix the brokenness would come through that great-great-great-great-grandkid who wouldn't be born for many more years. His name would be Jesus. While the world waited for Jesus, God would keep helping His special family to believe in His promise and to recover and pursue His awesome Plan.

CAN YOU THINK
OF A TIME WHEN YOU
MADE YOUR OWN PLAN
INSTEAD OF FOLLOWING
GOD'S PLAN?

4

Crazy Dreams

Genesis 37–50

The Plan

Time passed, and **God's special family began to grow, just like He said it would.** Isaac had two sons—Jacob and Esau—and Jacob had twelve sons, but his favorite son was Joseph. He gave Joseph special gifts, like a colorful robe. This special treatment made Joseph's brothers jealous, and they didn't like him very much.

The brothers also didn't like it when Joseph told them about his dreams. These weren't dreams about sheep jumping over fences. They were dreams about how Joseph would be greater and more successful than any of his brothers. Joseph dreamed that his brothers—and even his mom and dad—would one day serve him and bow down to him. His brothers were not thrilled at the idea of bowing down to Joseph. Even their dad, Jacob, questioned his son about it.

One day Joseph put on his fancy colorful coat and visited his older brothers in the fields. The coat reminded the brothers that Joseph was their father's favorite. When they saw him coming, they got angry and wanted to kill him! Thankfully, one of the brothers convinced the others to sell Joseph as a slave instead. They sold off Joseph and then lied to their dad, saying that a wild animal had killed him.

Joseph was scared, but he trusted that God had a Plan. He eventually ended up in Egypt working for a man named Potiphar. Even though Joseph was far from home, God's blessing was on him. Potiphar put Joseph in charge of his whole household. Things were going well until Potiphar's wife became angry at Joseph and told lies about him. Potiphar had Joseph thrown in jail!

THE FALL

THIS WAS THE SECOND TIME JOSEPH HAD ENDED UP SOMEWHERE HE DIDN'T WANT TO BE—OR DESERVE TO BE—BECAUSE OF SOMEONE ELSE'S SIN. But he still trusted that God had a Plan. And God did have a Plan. The prison guards could tell that God's blessing was on Joseph, so they put him in charge of the jail. Soon two other prisoners, a cupbearer and baker who both worked for Pharaoh (the ruler of Egypt), told Joseph they had been having crazy dreams. These guys didn't know what the dreams meant, and they were confused. God helped Joseph understand the dreams. Joseph said the cupbearer's dream meant he would soon be free from jail and working with Pharaoh again. Joseph asked the cupbearer to remember him and help get him out of jail too! But Joseph told the baker that he was in big trouble—Pharaoh was going to kill him.

Sure enough, Joseph was right. Soon the cupbearer was released and began working for Pharaoh again, and the baker lost his life. Joseph hoped the cupbearer would help him out of jail, but the cupbearer had forgotten all about Joseph. For two years Joseph waited in jail, trusting God had a Plan.

God had not forgotten Joseph. About this same time, it was Pharaoh's turn to have some crazy dreams . . . about skinny cows eating fat cows and thin grain eating fat grain. Pharaoh couldn't find anybody who could tell him the meaning of the dreams. When the cupbearer heard about Pharaoh's crazy dreams, he finally remembered Joseph. Maybe Joseph could help Pharaoh.

Soon Joseph was in front of the Egyptian king, explaining that God would allow Joseph to know what his dreams meant. Joseph listened to Pharaoh explain his crazy cow dream and his crazy grain dream. Then Joseph said the dreams meant there would be seven years of plentiful crops and food in abundance. Those seven years of plenty would be followed by seven years of drought and famine with no food. He told Pharaoh to set people in charge of gathering and storing food in the seven good years to prepare for the seven bad years. Pharaoh was really impressed with Joseph's plan. The king knew that God's blessing was on Joseph, so he put Joseph in charge of all Egypt, second only to Pharaoh himself.

Pharaoh's dreams all came true. When the seven bad years came, Egypt was the only place that was prepared, thanks to Joseph's leadership and God's blessing on him. People from all over traveled to Egypt for food. Some of those people were none other than Joseph's brothers! It had been many years since Joseph's brothers had sold him as a slave. Joseph had grown up and had on Egyptian clothes. He wasn't a scared little brother in a colorful coat anymore. He was a powerful leader in charge of an entire nation. The brothers did not recognize Joseph. So when they saw him, they bowed down before him, just like he dreamed when he was a boy! After playing a few tricks on them, he revealed to them that he was their brother Joseph. They were scared about what he might do to them, but Joseph forgave them. He not only forgave them, but he also hugged them and loved them and took care of them all. He brought his entire family to Egypt to live with him!

THE VERY GOOD NEWS

GOD RESCUED HIS SPECIAL FAMILY THROUGH JOSEPH. Joseph spent much of his life in brokenness because of other people's sins, but God took what others meant for bad and turned it into good. God still had a Plan. God's promise to bless the world and fix the brokenness would come through that great-great-great-great-grandkid who wouldn't be born for many more years. His name would be Jesus. While the world waited for Jesus, God would keep helping His special family to believe in His promise and to recover and pursue His awesome Plan.

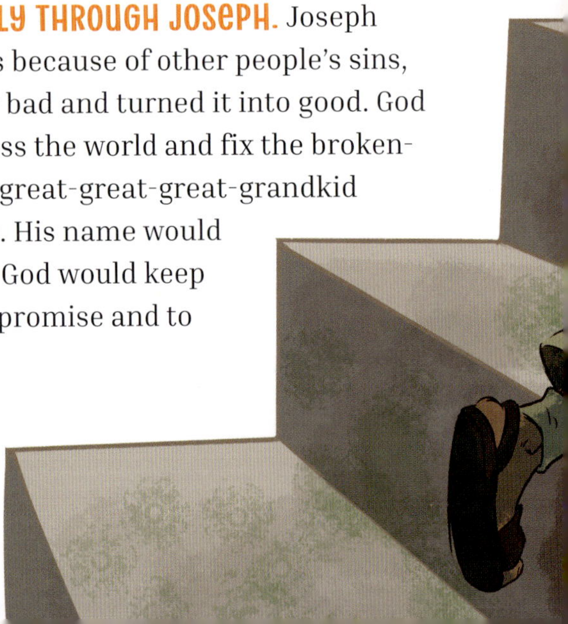

JOSEPH SAW A
LOT OF BROKENNESS!
WHY DO YOU THINK HE
WAS STILL ABLE TO
TRUST GOD?

5

The Ten Rules and a Shiny Cow

EXODUS 20–33

God's special family, the Israelites, were now living in Egypt because Joseph had saved his family from the famine. As time went on, the twelve brothers' families grew and grew. New pharaohs ruled the land and were scared that the growing number of Israelites might try to take over, so the pharaohs made the Israelites slaves. God's people cried out for deliverance for many years until God called a man named Moses to lead the people out of Egypt. God parted the Red Sea so His people could escape, and they headed toward the land God had promised to Abraham. On the way, God called Moses to climb a mountain to talk with Him. On the top of the mountain there was thunder and lightning, and the mountain was surrounded with a thick cloud.

THE PLAN

GOD TOLD MOSES HIS PLAN FOR HOW HIS PEOPLE SHOULD LIVE, HOW THEY SHOULD TREAT EACH OTHER, AND HOW THEY SHOULD WORSHIP HIM AND SET THEMSELVES APART FROM THE REST OF THE WORLD. God started with His Ten Commandments, written on two stone tablets, which summed up important basics such as only worship God, take a day off to rest, honor your mom and dad, and do not steal or lie. Then God began to explain some very specific things He wanted the Israelites to do. If the people obeyed, they would truly begin to recover and pursue life the way God planned it to be in the very beginning before sin led everything to brokenness.

While Moses was still on the mountain talking to God, the Israelites started to whine and complain. Moses was taking too long to return. They begged Aaron, Moses's brother, to make an idol they could worship. They didn't want a God who came in a cloud on top of a mountain. They wanted a god they could see with their own eyes. Aaron agreed and told everyone to bring him their gold earrings and jewelry. He used it all to make them a golden calf.

Once the golden calf was finished, the people began to sing and praise it. They even made a sacrifice to it! This made the true God—the one meeting with Moses on the mountain—really, really mad. God told Moses He was going to punish the Israelites even though they were His special people. God was going to wipe them out and start over again. Moses pleaded with God to spare them, not for their own sake, but so the Egyptians would know the Israelites were God's people. God listened to Moses and sent him to speak to the people.

As Moses climbed down the mountain with the two stone tablets in his arms, he heard joyful singing. When he finished the long walk down, he couldn't believe his eyes. **There, in the middle of the people, was a golden calf. God's people were dancing and singing around it.** They were worshiping the idol like it was a god, even though they had just seen Aaron make it! Now it was Moses's turn to be angry. He smashed the two stone tablets on the ground and had the golden calf burned in the fire. Then he took the melted gold out of the fire, ground it up into a powder, threw it in the water, and made the people drink it. He was mad!

THE FALL

Moses called the Israelites to repent of their sins. They needed to change their hearts and be sorry for what they had done. Moses went back up the mountain to talk to God. He asked God to forgive the people. God said He would once again write His Plan on two tablets so the people could see it and follow it.

Then Moses asked to see God's glory, but God knew Moses could not see God's full glory and still live. So God told Moses to stand in a crack in the rocks. Then God covered Moses with His hand and let Moses see His back. **THE VERY GOOD NEWS: GOD RENEWED HIS PROMISE TO HIS PEOPLE—THE PROMISE TO SAVE THEM AND TO BLESS THE WORLD THROUGH THEM, DESPITE THEIR SIN.** God still wanted them to recover and pursue His Plan.

Once again, Moses picked up the stone tablets and went down the mountain to explain God's Plan to the Israelites. But this time something happened that had never happened before. Moses's face was glowing! His face shone from that small glimpse of God's back.

For the next forty years, Moses would speak to God and lead the Israelites through the wilderness toward the Promised Land. He would teach them about God's Plan. God's forgiveness was good news. God's glory was good news. The Promised Land was good news. But the best news of all was still to come.

WHY DO YOU THINK GOD WANTED TO SHARE HIS PLAN WITH HIS PEOPLE?

6

SPIES, RED ROPE, AND SHOUTING

JOSHUA 2 AND 6

Moses led the Israelites around the wilderness for forty years. When he died, his right-hand man, Joshua, took over as leader. God told Joshua to be strong and courageous because he would lead the people into the Promised Land (also called the land of Canaan). **GOD'S PLAN FOR ISRAEL WAS FOR THEM TO CONQUER THE PEOPLE WHO ALREADY LIVED IN CANAAN.** Some of the Canaanites lived in big cities with strong walls. The fight was going to be tough. But God promised that He would fight for His people. Joshua was fired up, ready to fight, and ready to follow God's Plan.

THE PLAN

The first major city the Israelites came to was Jericho, which was surrounded by towering walls. Joshua knew it would be a very difficult—if not impossible—city to conquer, so he sent two spies to sneak into the city and report to him on what to expect. The spies snooped around and gathered information about Jericho.

While in Jericho, the spies stayed with a woman named Rahab. Rahab ran a business out of her home, kind of like a hotel. She was a Canaanite, so she didn't know the true God or know about His Plan. **SO RAHAB DIDN'T HONOR GOD WITH HER BUSINESS, AND SHE MADE LOTS OF SINFUL DECISIONS.** Her life was a mess. Without God in her life, Rahab had no hope. Even though she didn't know it yet, God loved her and was going to turn her life around.

THE FALL

Lots of people were always coming and going from Rahab's house, so it was the perfect spot for the spies to go unnoticed. Unfortunately, the king of Jericho found out about the spies' secret mission and wasn't too happy about them sneaking around his city. He sent soldiers to find and capture the two sneaky Israelites. The spies needed a place to hide—and quick! So Rahab hid the men on the roof by covering them with bundles of flax from the fields.

When the soldiers arrived at Rahab's house, they told her to bring out the men from Israel and turn them over to the king. But Rahab was a quick thinker. She said the men had just left and that if the soldiers hurried, they might catch up with them! As soon as the soldiers heard this, they headed out of the city in a cloud of dust. Rahab climbed to the roof to tell the spies the coast was clear. She told them she had heard all the great things their God had done for His people in the wilderness and all the battles they had won with the Lord's help. Rahab believed that their God was the true God. Even though she had sinned a lot, Rahab wanted to follow the true God, like the Israelites. She wanted to be a part of God's Plan.

Rahab's house was on the outer wall of the city, so she threw a red rope out her window so that the spies could climb down and leave the city to safety. Rahab knew the Israelite army was going to conquer Jericho. She asked the spies to spare her family's lives when their army attacked, just as she had saved the two men's lives that day. The spies agreed and gave her very specific instructions. She needed to tie that same red rope on her window so their army could see it when they came. If she did this, everyone in her house would be safe. Then the spies climbed down the rope and rushed back to Joshua with their report.

Soon God told Joshua how the Israelites would take over Jericho. They would march around it one time each day for six days. On the seventh day, they would march around seven times and then shout and blow trumpets. The first day, they marched around Jericho one time. The Bible doesn't say, but maybe the two spies looked up and saw the red rope hanging from Rahab's window. Day two, the same. Days three, four, five, and six, the same. Each day the spies might have seen the red rope, and each day Rahab and her family hoped God would save them. Then it was day seven. The Israelites marched around seven times. Rahab trusted the spies and trusted God. She believed they would keep their promise.

After the army marched around the city a seventh time, Joshua yelled, the people shouted, and the priests blew their trumpets as hard as they could. They all felt a rumble. They saw cracks creeping up the walls, and rock and mortar began to fall. In the blink of an eye those famous, defensive walls crumbled to the ground. As the dust and debris settled, God's army charged

in to take over the city. But the two spies likely looked over and saw one small part of the outer wall still standing, and from a window they saw a red rope swaying in the wind. Rahab and her family were safe and sound, just as the spies had promised.

For the rest of her life, Rahab lived as one of the Israelites and understood that God's promises are good news. **GOD SHOWED HER GRACE AND SAVED HER FROM HER BROKEN AND MESSY LIFE.** He allowed Rahab to recover and pursue His Plan for her life. God's love for Rahab shows that God's promises and God's Plan aren't just for Israelites; they are for all kinds of people—and that means *you*!

THE VERY GOOD NEWS

Hundreds of years later, a boy would be born who was Rahab's great-great-great-great—lots of greats—grandson. His name was Jesus, and He was the answer to the promise God had given to bless the world and fix all the brokenness. Jesus made all God's promises come true.

WHO DO YOU KNOW WHO NEEDS TO HEAR ABOUT GOD'S PROMISES AND GOD'S PLAN?

7

GIRL POWER

JUDGES 4–5

Joshua led the Israelites into the Promised Land. Of course God wanted His people to follow His Plan for their lives. But when Joshua died, no one took his place. Without a leader, the Israelites had a hard time listening to God. They ignored God's Plan and began to sin a lot and do things their own way. So God allowed different kings and nations to rule over His people. God was trying to get their attention. After years of being oppressed, the Israelites finally called to God to deliver them and to fix the brokenness they felt from their sins.

THE PLAN

GOD HEARD THEM AND GAVE THEM SPECIAL LEADERS CALLED JUDGES WHO WOULD POINT THE PEOPLE BACK TO GOD AND HIS PLAN FOR THEIR LIVES. One of these judges was named Deborah.

Deborah was a very wise woman who spoke with God and delivered His message to the people. When she became a judge, the Canaanites were the bad guys oppressing God's people. The leader of the Canaanites was a cruel man named Sisera, who commanded a powerful army of iron chariots. Everyone was scared to stand up against Sisera's army.

One day Deborah had an important meeting with a man named Barak, the general of the Israelite army. Deborah told Barak that God wanted him to attack Sisera and his army. She told Barak that God would make the Israelites victorious, but Barak had a hard time trusting God. He did know that God was always with Deborah, so he said he would fight only if Deborah helped him lead the army. Deborah agreed to go with Barak into battle against cruel Sisera. But because Barak wouldn't trust God for himself, Deborah said Barak would not be the one to kill Sisera. God would let a woman kill Sisera instead!

Sisera's iron chariots were ready. The battle was coming, and both armies were prepared to fight.

Barak knew his army didn't stand a chance against Sisera and his chariots. He had to believe that God was in control and would deliver His people . . . and that's what God did! Once the battle started, God brought a great storm on the battlefield. The rain from God's storm overflowed the nearby river, and Sisera's big, scary chariots got stuck in the mud. Barak and his men charged forward and began to win the fight. Knowing he was losing the battle, Sisera jumped from his chariot and ran away. He left his entire army behind. All of them were killed.

THE FALL

SISERA RAN AND RAN—HE WAS RUNNING FOR HIS LIFE. He finally got tired and stopped at the tent of a woman named Jael. Jael's family was friendly with the Canaanites. Sisera was glad to see a friendly face because he needed her help. Sisera knew that Barak and the Israelites were trying to find him. He needed a place to hide, and Jael invited him in.

Sisera was exhausted after a hard day of battle that hadn't gone the way he had planned. Jael gave him some milk and made a place for him to sleep on the floor. Before he fell asleep, Sisera told Jael to stand guard and tell anyone who came looking for him that he wasn't there. She agreed, and Sisera fell asleep, probably dreaming of a plan to defeat Barak and his army.

But while Sisera slept peacefully, Jael quietly grabbed a long tent peg and her hammer. Normally, she used these to secure her tent from blowing away, but today they were for something different. She tiptoed over to the sleeping Sisera and held the peg to his head. She raised the hammer high and swung it down with all her strength. *Wham!* And that was the end of Sisera.

WHEN WE DON'T KNOW GOD'S PLAN FOR OUR LIVES, HOW CAN WE STILL TRUST HIM?

Soon Barak arrived, looking for Sisera and ready to fight. But surprise! Sisera was already dead. When Barak saw him, he remembered how Deborah had told him that a woman would be the one to kill Sisera. The Canaanites were defeated, and the Israelites were saved. God had kept His promises and rescued His people again!

Barak and Deborah sang a wonderful song of praise about God's victory. Deborah would lead God's people for forty great years of rest and peace. **HER STORY REMINDS US THAT GOD USES MEN AND WOMEN, BOYS AND GIRLS AS PART OF HIS PLAN. AND THAT MEANS GOD CAN USE *YOU*!**

THE VERY GOOD NEWS

Sadly, after Deborah died, the Israelites turned away from God in disobedience once again. They were mistreated by kings and nations, they kept sinning, and they ended up in brokenness time after time. The cycle would keep repeating for many, many years. But even though God's people turned away from Him, God always called them back. God loves His people no matter what. And one day God would send a leader who would rescue His people once and for all.

8

OFF WITH HIS HEAD

1 SAMUEL 17

During the time of the judges, the Israelites were in a downward spiral of disobedience and brokenness. The people went further and further from God's Plan for them. After many, many years, and many, many judges, the people cried out to God and asked Him for a king. They wanted a king so they could be like all the other nations around them. Back then, every nation had a king or a queen. **BUT GOD WANTED HIS PEOPLE TO BE DIFFERENT. HE WANTED THEM TO SEE *HIM* AS THEIR KING.**

THE PLAN

The Israelites continued to beg, "Give us a king! Give us a king!" So God finally gave them what they wanted. Their first king was named Saul. King Saul didn't start off as a bad king, but he didn't lead the people with God-given courage. As King Saul got older, he got further and further away from God's Plan.

One of the nations in Canaan at the time was the Philistines. These guys were really tough and really mean. They hated God, and they hated God's people. So it's no surprise that the Israelites were constantly at war with the Philistines. Everyone in Israel, including King Saul, was scared of them. Why? It wasn't just because of the number of Philistine soldiers or their weapons or their strategy. The Israelites were mostly scared because of one Philistine—Goliath.

Goliath was tall—like, really, really tall . . . over 9 feet tall with bulging muscles. His armor weighed 125 pounds, and his spear was fit for a giant. Every Israelite soldier had heard stories about the mighty and terrifying Goliath.

The Israelite and Philistine armies were on opposite sides of a valley, looking across at each other and getting ready to fight. If Goliath's height, strength, and weapons weren't intimidating enough, every morning he would roar across the valley, challenging the Israelites to a one-on-one battle. "Pick your best fighter!" Goliath would say. "We will fight to the death—winner take all!" Goliath would make fun of Israel, and he would make fun of God.

But nobody in the Israelite army was willing to fight Goliath. For forty days the giant's shouts echoed through the valley. The Israelites *should* have trusted God. **THE FALL** **They *should* have believed in God's Plan and been brave because they *should* have known that God was with them and would fight for them. But instead the Israelites shook with fear.**

One day a boy named David came to visit his three older brothers who were soldiers. David was only a teenager. He saw the fear in everyone's eyes, and he heard the mocking voice from across the valley. Goliath was taunting the Israelites and calling them scaredy cats. Worst of all, David heard Goliath making fun of God as all the soldiers shook with fear.

David was mad. How dare that Philistine make fun of God and God's people! Even though David was a shepherd boy, not a battle-tested warrior, he had learned to protect his sheep from wild animals. And David had great faith in God. David had killed a lion and a bear that had attacked his sheep, and he knew God had helped him both times. So now David told King Saul that he would fight the giant and God would help him once again! King Saul agreed to let David fight Goliath. He insisted David wear the king's armor. David tried it on, but it was way too big for a scrawny shepherd boy. Instead he picked up five smooth stones and his slingshot. David trusted God and believed in God's Plan. He was brave because he knew God would fight for him.

As David entered the valley, so did Goliath. When the giant saw that David was just a boy with a staff and some stones, he asked if David thought the giant was a dog to come at him with a little stick. But David said that even though Goliath was fighting with a sword and spear, David was fighting in the name of the Lord. He knew that once Goliath was dead, everyone would know that God is the one true King who fights for the Israelites.

This enraged Goliath, who charged at David to kill him. Instead of running away, David took out one of the smooth stones, placed it in his sling, ran toward the giant, and flung the stone toward Goliath. Bull's-eye. The stone hit Goliath right in the forehead. He instantly stumbled and fell face first to the ground. *Bam!*

David stepped onto the giant's back, raised the giant's huge sword up high, and chopped off Goliath's head so that everyone watching would know for sure that the mighty giant was dead. The Philistines ran away in fear, and the Israelites chased after them in victory, all because of a shepherd boy's faith in God.

THE VERY GOOD NEWS

David would eventually replace Saul as Israel's king. **GOD WOULD USE THIS SHEPHERD BOY—A MAN AFTER GOD'S OWN HEART—TO RESCUE THE PEOPLE AND LEAD THEM TO RECOVER AND PURSUE GOD'S PLAN.** David was a great fighter, a great rescuer, and a great king. But David wasn't perfect. Even with him in charge, Israel still failed to follow God's Plan. One day, one of David's great-great-great—lots of greats again—grandsons would be born, and His name would be Jesus. Jesus would fight for God's people, rescue them, and be the greatest King of all. And Jesus would show the whole world what God's Plan was all about.

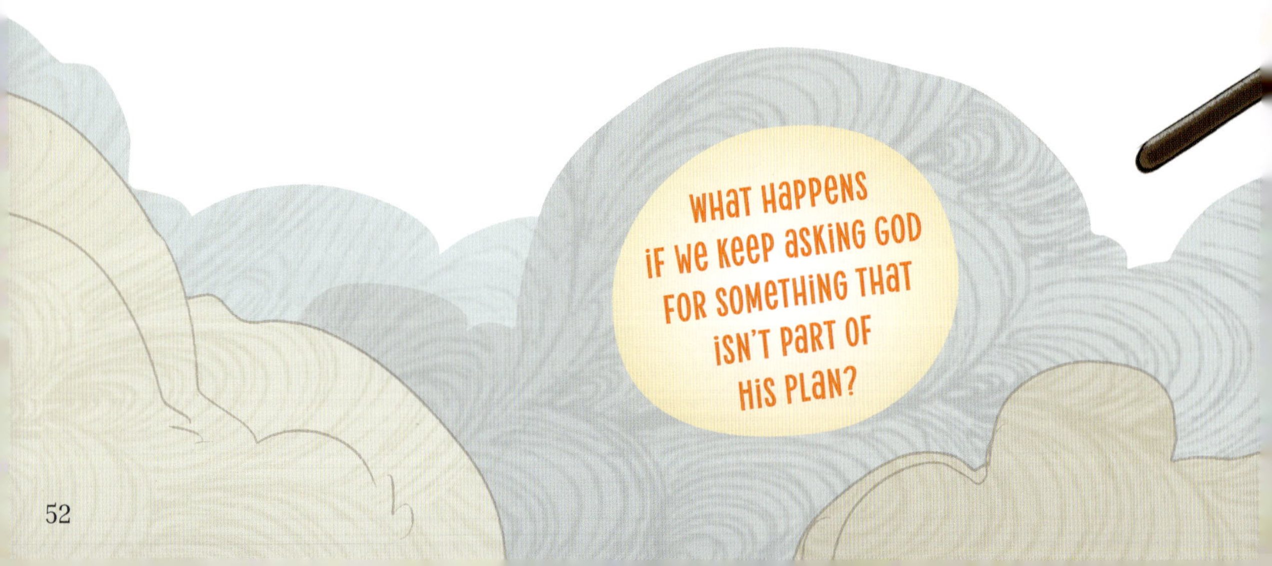

9

FIRE FALLING FROM THE SKY

1 KINGS 18

King David ruled over Israel and helped the people follow God's Plan. When David died, there were ups and downs and, finally, a civil war that split the land into two kingdoms—Israel to the north and Judah to the south. The kingdoms drifted away from worshiping God and began to worship false gods.

In Israel, Ahab became king. He and his wife, Jezebel, did not worship God or follow His Plan. They led the people to worship Baal, the false god. Queen Jezebel even had the prophets of the one true God hunted and killed!

Elijah was a prophet of God. Back in those days **GOD USED A PROPHET (OR A PROPHETESS, IF IT WAS A WOMAN) TO SPEAK TO THE KINGS OF ISRAEL AND JUDAH.** God would tell the prophet what to say. Sometimes God's messages would tell the future: "There is going to be a war!" Sometimes God's messages would be warnings: "You guys are about to get in trouble." But all of God's messages were encouraging: "God still loves you, and He won't give up on you!"

THE PLAN

God sent Elijah to confront evil Ahab. Elijah told Ahab that because he and Jezebel wouldn't follow God's Plan, God wasn't going to let it rain anymore in Israel. Ahab knew if there was no rain, there would be no food and the people would be hungry. Hungry people get mad. And Ahab knew the people would be mad at him! So Ahab and Jezebel were in big trouble.

Ahab blamed Elijah for stopping the rain even though it was really King Ahab and Jezebel's fault. Instead of changing their hearts, repenting, and asking the true God for help, **THE KING AND QUEEN PRAYED TO THE FALSE GOD BAAL. INSTEAD OF LISTENING TO ELIJAH—THE PROPHET OF THE TRUE GOD—AHAB AND JEZEBEL LISTENED TO THE PROPHETS OF BAAL.** (Yes, false gods had prophets too.) And worst of all, the people of Israel started doing the same thing.

THE FALL

Elijah knew God wanted to teach Ahab and Jezebel a lesson. He told king Ahab to meet him on Mount Carmel along with all 450 prophets of Baal and the people of Israel. King Ahab agreed.

At Mount Carmel, Elijah told the people they had to choose between Baal and God. He challenged the 450 prophets of Baal to a contest to see who was the true God so the people would know which god to worship. Elijah gave

these rules: (1) Kill a bull to be sacrificed. (2) Place the meat on an altar with wood on top, but do not light it on fire. (3) Pray to your god and ask him to set fire to the sacrifice. The god who sent fire would be the one true God who deserved their worship.

The prophets of Baal went first. They cried out to Baal to send fire, but nothing happened. They hollered all morning. Nothing. They danced around the altar, shouting. Still nothing. Elijah began to make fun of them: "Maybe Baal is using the bathroom! Or maybe he's out of town! Or maybe he's taking a nap! You should yell louder and wake him up!" The prophets of Baal began to go crazy, shouting louder and louder, cutting themselves with swords. They wanted to prove they were serious about their false gods. They continued all afternoon, and still nothing. No voice from the sky. No sparks. Absolutely nothing happened. So the prophets of Baal gave up. They must have been embarrassed!

Now it was Elijah's turn. He built an altar of twelve stones representing the twelve tribes of Israel. Then he dug a trench around the altar, like a moat around a castle. He placed a sacrifice to God on the altar. Finally, he had twelve jars of water dumped on the altar so that the wood and meat were completely soaked and water filled up the trench. There was no way Elijah himself could have lit a fire!

Elijah looked to heaven and prayed. He asked God to prove He was the one true God and to show He would help His people to follow His Plan again. When Elijah's prayer ended, flames poured out of the sky! In an instant, the meat, the wood, the stones, the dust, and even the water were completely consumed. All that stood before Elijah was a burnt ditch.

When the people saw what had happened, they fell on their faces to worship God. They repented from their sins and believed in their hearts that He was indeed the one true God.

Elijah told the people to turn back to God and worship Him only. God had sent fire to show He was still their God. He wanted to forgive them, restore them, and bless them. He had a good Plan for them. For a short time the people of Israel repented and turned back to God. But sadly, it wasn't long before they turned away again. The people continued to sin and leave the Plan God had for them.

THE VERY GOOD NEWS

BUT GOD NEVER GAVE UP ON HIS PEOPLE. One day there would be another sacrifice, only this time it would be a man, God's own Son. Instead of fire being poured out on the sacrifice, God's wrath would be poured out on His own Son. That sacrifice would create the only way out of the brokenness caused by sin. That one sacrifice would change everything. And that's Very Good News!

WHY DO YOU
THINK THE ISRAELITES
CHOSE SIN AND
BROKENNESS INSTEAD
OF GOD'S PLAN?

10

SOMETHING SMELLS FISHY

JONAH 1–4

While God's family was split into two kingdoms, He sent many prophets to warn His people and encourage them to follow His Plan. One was the prophet Jonah, who lived in Israel. **GOD TOLD JONAH TO GO TO THE CITY OF NINEVEH AND WARN THE PEOPLE THAT THEY WOULD BE DESTROYED IF THEY DID NOT TURN TO GOD.** Jonah didn't like this idea very much. In fact, he hated it. The Ninevites were ruthless and selfish and the enemies of the Israelites. Jonah knew if he warned the Ninevites and they decided to repent and follow God's Plan, God would forgive them and restore them and bless them. Jonah didn't think the Ninevites deserved the chance to be forgiven and restored and blessed. So Jonah ran.

THE PLAN

No one knows why Jonah thought he could run away from God, but he tried. He bought a ticket for a boat sailing in the opposite direction from Nineveh. Jonah got on the boat, lay down, and went to sleep. He thought he could sail away into the sunset, but that's not how God works. God pursues His people. While Jonah was snoring in the bottom of the boat, a great storm appeared out of nowhere, throwing the boat this way and that, up and down, side to side. If the boat sank, everyone on board would drown. The panicked sailors began tossing everything they could overboard to help stop the boat from sinking! And the whole time, Jonah was asleep. Eventually, the angry captain found Jonah sleeping. He commanded Jonah to call out to his God to stop this ferocious storm.

The sailors realized that the storm was God getting Jonah's attention. But why was God so mad at Jonah? Jonah explained that he worshiped the one true God but that he had disobeyed God and was running away. The sailors were terrified because they had heard stories about what the God of the Israelites was able to do. They asked Jonah how to stop God's anger. Jonah's answer didn't make them very happy; he said they had to throw him overboard into the sea!

At first, the sailors refused. They tried their best to row back to shore, but water was pouring over the sides and threatening to sink them all. Soon they realized there was only one option. They looked to heaven and asked God to forgive them. They grabbed Jonah, and . . . *splash!* Jonah was in the sea. The instant Jonah's body touched the sea, the storm stopped. The wind, the rain, the waves—all were calm, and Jonah started to sink under the water. Then a big shadow came up from the depths. The shadow approached Jonah's sinking body—it was a huge fish! The fish opened its mouth and swallowed Jonah whole.

Jonah opened his eyes and could only see darkness. We can imagine that he gasped for air and smelled only nastiness. He felt around trying to figure out where he was. Everything was squishy and gross. Jonah realized he was in the belly of a fish. **HE SPENT THE NEXT THREE DAYS AND THREE NIGHTS CALLING THAT FISH BELLY HOME. JONAH FELT BROKEN.** There in the dark, stinky, squishy fish belly, God finally got Jonah's attention.

THE FALL

Jonah prayed. He asked God to forgive him and give him another chance. God heard Jonah and told the fish to spit Jonah out. The huge fish swam toward land, popped its big head out of the water, and threw up on the beach. And out came Jonah.

Jonah opened his eyes again and saw bright light. He gasped, and the salty air filled his lungs. He realized he was back on dry ground! God spoke to Jonah again. For the second time, He told the prophet to go to Nineveh and warn the people to repent and follow God's Plan or be destroyed. Now Jonah was ready to go, so he stood up and began the journey to Nineveh.

Jonah entered the city. He probably smelled like fish and looked pretty icky, but he gave the Ninevites God's message nonetheless. And do you know what happened? Every single person in the city, including the king, listened. They all repented and asked God to forgive them of their sins. God heard them, forgave them, restored them, and blessed them.

This made Jonah extremely mad and pouty. He whined to God, but **GOD EVEN HAD PATIENCE WITH JONAH. GOD REMINDED JONAH THAT HE LOVES ALL KINDS OF PEOPLE,** and only God can help them find a way out of their brokenness. The Ninevites weren't the only people God wanted to rescue from brokenness. God wanted to rescue all kinds of people all over the world. But it would take more than a flawed prophet like Jonah to save them. It would take the perfect prophet, the Son of God, who would run to the people, not away from them. He would die in their place so they could be forgiven, restored, and blessed by God. And *that* is the Very Good News.

THE VERY GOOD NEWS

God made sure the Ninevites had a way out of brokenness. What has He done to show *you* the way?

11

The Kid Who Became King

2 Chronicles 34–35

Many years had passed since King David ruled over Israel. Kings had come and gone, and most of them completely ignored God's Plan and tried to do things their own way instead. God's people experienced a lot of brokenness. This went on for years and years, king after king, until most of God's people didn't even look like God's people anymore. Instead of being different and unique (in a good way), they were acting like all the nations around them. They were worshiping false gods and idols. They had forgotten God's laws and His beautiful Plan for their lives.

One day in the middle of all this brokenness, an eight-year-old boy named Josiah was crowned king of Judah! Something was different about him, and it wasn't just that he was a kid king. Josiah loved God and wanted to lead his people to worship the true God again instead of false gods and idols. **The young king wanted the people to remember God's Plan.**

The Plan

When Josiah was about twenty years old, he traveled across his kingdom. During his trip, he was determined to destroy everything that had to do with false gods. He burned all the wooden idols. He broke the metal images into tiny pieces and tore down the altars made for sacrificing to false gods. King Josiah wanted to make sure everybody in the kingdom knew there was only one God worth worshiping.

A few years later, King Josiah decided it was time to rebuild the temple of God that his grandfather King Solomon had built. The temple was in rough shape. No one had been taking care of it, and it needed a lot of repairs. King Josiah hired workers and paid for the materials. Rebuilding the temple was a huge project! A priest named Hilkiah helped Josiah organize the work. One day, while cleaning out a storage room, Hilkiah found something incredibly special and important—the Book of the Law of the Lord. That book contained all the most important stories about God's special family as well as God's instructions for following His Plan. The book Hilkiah found is still a part of the Old Testament in our Bible!

When King Josiah heard about the Book of the Law, he had someone read the book to him. Maybe they read the first story ever about how God had planned everything the way it was supposed to be. Maybe they read about Adam and Eve and their sin and then how God sent a flood to wash the earth clean. Maybe they read about the Israelites rebelling again. King Josiah heard about God's love and God's desire to restore His people when they were in brokenness. He heard the commands God had given to help His people follow His Plan. **THE MORE KING JOSIAH HEARD, THE WORSE HE FELT. HE FELT SO BAD THAT HE TORE HIS ROYAL GARMENTS AND CRIED.**

THE FALL

Josiah cried because in the Book of the Law, God warned His people that if they didn't follow God's Plan, they would get into big trouble. God loved His people, and because He loved them, there were consequences when they failed to follow His Plan. Josiah wanted the people to pay attention and to remember, love, and honor God. Once Josiah read the Book, he knew that he and his people had not been following God's Plan. In fact, they deserved big trouble. He knew that if they wanted God to forgive them and restore them and bless them, some things were going to have to change.

God knew Josiah needed help figuring out what to do next. So God sent a prophetess named Huldah to help the king know what to do. Remember that back in those days, a prophet or prophetess gave messages from God to the king and the people. Huldah had a message for King Josiah. She said, "This is what God says: 'I will bring disaster and all the consequences that are in the book you heard because the people have forgotten about me and worshiped false gods and idols.' You have made God really angry." But Huldah also had some good news for the king: God would not punish the people while Josiah was king because Josiah repented and believed in God.

THE VERY GOOD NEWS

When King Josiah heard this message, he was excited. He gathered all the leaders, priests, and people to read to them the entire Book of God's Law. **JOSIAH LED GOD'S PEOPLE TO RECOVER AND PURSUE GOD'S PLAN.**

Even though King Josiah had a good heart, he still made a lot of mistakes. Sadly, after Josiah died, the people turned away from the one true God again. Soon the kingdom was right back into brokenness. But this isn't the end of the story. One day God was going to send another kid-King into the world. And that kid-King would grow up, obey God, and follow God's Plan in every way. The good news is that God still had His Plan to fix the problem of brokenness once and for all.

WHEN WE HAVEN'T FOLLOWED GOD'S PLAN BUT WE HUMBLY ASK FOR HIS FORGIVENESS, WHAT DOES HE DO?

12

Here, Kitty, Kitty

Daniel 6

Remember that God's people were split into two kingdoms, Israel and Judah. Because the people kept turning away from God and His Plan for their lives, God allowed them to be conquered by some of the most powerful nations on earth. Some of the Israelites were taken captive by the nations that conquered them. Over time, many of the Israelites (who were also called Jews) became just like the nations who had captured them. Once again, God's people began to worship and follow false gods.

But Daniel was one Jewish man who stayed faithful to God and His Plan. Daniel was a wise man and a hard worker, and God blessed him. Over the years, Daniel worked for many kings and held many high positions. One of the kings was King Darius.

King Darius had given Daniel a big job as the boss of important people. The king trusted Daniel so much that he planned to put Daniel in charge of everyone in the entire kingdom. The king could sit back and relax because he could trust Daniel to do the work!

But some men who worked with Daniel were extremely jealous of how much the king liked him. They snooped around trying to catch Daniel making a mistake or doing something wrong so they could get him in trouble. But no luck—Daniel was always faithful and always did what was right, even when no one was looking. The only part about Daniel's life they thought they could use against him was his devotion to God. **Daniel prayed to God every single day, three times a day.** These bad men made a plan to get Daniel in trouble because of his faithfulness to the one true God.

THE PLAN

Back in those days, many kings liked to think of themselves as gods. They loved to have people honor them and bow down to them and sing songs to them and even pray to them. The bad men told King Darius their idea for a great new law. The new law said that since King Darius was such an amazing and powerful man, the people should pray only to King Darius for thirty days. Well, King Darius thought people praying to him was the best idea ever! He immediately signed the law. In those days when a king signed a law, no one—not even the king—could change it. The bad men knew that Daniel would not keep this rule. He would only pray to his God and never to King Darius. The bad men ran off, giddy with excitement that their plan was going to work.

Daniel heard about the new law but knew he couldn't follow it. Just like every other day, he continued to kneel down and pray to the one true God. The jealous men spied on Daniel and saw him doing exactly what they knew he would do—praying to his God. They ran to King Darius to tell on Daniel! They told the king they saw Daniel praying to his God instead of King Darius. Then they reminded the king that the punishment for breaking the law was to be thrown into the lions' den!

When King Darius heard all this, he was miserable because Daniel was his friend. He tried to think of a way to save Daniel, but there was no way. With a heavy heart, King Darius ordered Daniel to be thrown into the lions' den. As the den was opened and Daniel was about to be thrown in, King Darius told him that he hoped his God would protect him. **AND THEN DANIEL WAS THROWN INTO THE LIONS' DEN.** That night the king could not eat or sleep. All he could do was think about Daniel and hope he would survive.

THE FALL

Early the next morning the king rushed to the lions' den and cried out to Daniel, asking if Daniel's God—the one true God—had saved him from the lions. And then Daniel responded! He told King Darius that God had kept him safe! He had spent the night with the lions like they were little kitty cats. Daniel had faithfully followed God, and God had saved him! The king was relieved that his friend was unharmed. But his relief quickly turned to rage. He called for the jealous men and threw *them* into the lions' den. After spending the night *not* eating Daniel, those lions were probably hungry!

King Darius was so amazed that the one true God had saved Daniel from lions that he issued a new law that everyone should believe in Daniel's God. **The king realized that the only way Daniel could have been saved from the lions was if God had rescued Him.** God loves to rescue His people. One day, God would send His Son to rescue His people from their sins once and for all. God knew that some would reject His Son just as the jealous men had rejected Daniel. But others, like King Darius, would believe and repent of their sins. One day, but not quite yet.

The Very Good News

WHY DO YOU THINK PART OF GOD'S PLAN IS THAT WE WORSHIP ONLY HIM?

13

THE MOST BEAUTIFUL QUEEN

ESTHER 1–5, 7–8

When the Jewish people were captured by other nations, they were taken far from Israel. Thousands and thousands of Jews settled in new cities. They got jobs, built houses, had children, and began to think of these other nations as their true homes. Mordecai and Esther were two of those people. They were cousins, but Mordecai was quite a bit older. After Esther's parents died, Mordecai had raised her like his own daughter. Their grandparents had been taken captive many years before. Now their family lived in Susa, the capital of the Persian Empire. Even though God's people were living in a foreign land, He had not forgotten about them. **GOD HAD A PLAN TO BRING HIS PEOPLE HOME AND A PLAN TO USE ESTHER IN AN INCREDIBLE WAY.**

THE PLAN

Susa was the home of the Persian king Xerxes, who was a little crazy. One night during a party that had already lasted six months, the king asked his wife the queen to get dressed up so everyone at the party could see how pretty she was. His wife refused. The king (remember we said he was crazy) got so mad that he kicked the queen out of the castle!

Later, Xerxes was lonely and began a search for a new queen. All the most attractive, single women in the kingdom were brought to Susa for a massive beauty contest. The plan was for Xerxes to choose his favorite as the new queen. Esther was stunningly beautiful. She was taken to the king's court, and when King Xerxes met Esther, he crowned her queen! But he didn't know Esther was a Jew.

One day Mordecai was standing by the gate to the king's court when an important man named Haman passed through. Haman worked for King Xerxes and was so important that everyone was supposed to bow to him. On this particular day, all the people around the gate bowed to Haman except Mordecai. Haman was insulted. And Haman got mad. From that day on, he plotted to get revenge not only on Mordecai but also on all of Mordecai's people—the Jews. Haman convinced King Xerxes that the Jews were a problem, like an infestation of bugs. **He told the king the Jews needed to be exterminated.** The crazy king agreed! He signed a law that a few months later, all the Jews in the kingdom would be killed.

THE FALL

When Mordecai heard about the law, he sent word to Esther. Even though the king didn't know Esther was a Jew, her life was at stake, as were the lives of all her people. Mordecai told her to go see the king and ask him to change the law. Esther was afraid. No one was allowed to just walk into the court. If the king had not invited you, and he wasn't happy to see you, then he could have you killed. Plus, everyone knew the king was crazy.

But Mordecai encouraged Esther to be brave and told her that maybe Esther had become queen for that very moment in time, to save herself and her people. So she decided to bravely visit the king. And if she died, she died.

Esther must have been nervous. She didn't know if the king would be mad or glad when she showed up. She dressed in her royal clothes and went in to see him. When the king saw Esther, he wasn't mad at all. He was thrilled. Xerxes was so glad to see Esther that he offered her anything in the whole kingdom. Esther could have just asked Xerxes to rescue the Jews then and there, but she had a plan. She asked Xerxes to come to a dinner party and asked Haman to come too. The two men eagerly agreed. At dinner, the king and Haman had such a good time that Xerxes again offered Esther anything she wanted in the whole kingdom. To the king's surprise, Esther simply invited him and Haman to another dinner party the next day. They agreed to come; the king loved parties!

At dinner the next night, the king asked Esther again what she wanted. Esther announced she wanted him to save her life and her people's lives. The king was confused. Esther reminded Xerxes of Haman's law that all the Jews should be killed. She told him she was a Jew! So Haman's law meant she would have to die as well. The king was really, really upset and left the room, angry at Haman. He had to think about what to do. Haman realized he was in big trouble.

While Xerxes was outside, Haman begged Esther to save him. At that moment, the king returned and saw Haman way too close to the queen. The king thought Haman was trying to hurt Esther. Now the crazy king was furious! He ordered Haman killed immediately.

The king gave all Haman's stuff—his house and money—to Queen Esther. Then he gave Haman's important position to Mordecai. The king also wrote a new law that saved the Jews and punished anyone who hurt or killed them. **God had used brave Esther to save His people again. When you read the Bible, you see that God uses all kinds of people.** And you see that God works in really unusual ways! He can even use beauty queens and dinner parties.

The Very Good News

A few hundred years later, a Jew would be born who would go before the one true King on behalf of all people. This Jew, named Jesus, would save His people from death and remind them that this world is not their true home.

14

A Very Special Baby

Matthew 1; Luke 1

God had been silent for four hundred years. No prophets spoke. No miracles happened. No angels visited with special messages. Many of God's people wandered away from His Plan, but others waited for Him to send the special baby who would grow up, follow God's Plan, forgive their sins, and fix their brokenness. Then one day, the silence was broken. God sent an angel to visit a young woman who was about to get married. The woman's name was Mary.

Mary was frightened when she saw the angel in all his brilliance. The angel told her not to be afraid because God was pleased with her. He had chosen her for a very special assignment. **SHE WAS GOING TO HAVE A BABY, BUT NOT JUST ANY BABY. THIS BABY WAS GOD'S SON, AND HE WOULD BE THE SAVIOR OF THE WORLD.** Confusion filled Mary's head because she wasn't married and didn't know how she could be the Savior's mom. The angel comforted her and told Mary that God would be with her through it all. So, Mary trusted God. She began to think about what it would be like to be the mom of the one they had been waiting for since Adam and Eve were kicked out of the garden because of their sin. She would be the mom of the one who would fix the Fall and make a way out of the brokenness. The angel told her to name the baby *Jesus*.

THE PLAN

The angel also visited Joseph, Mary's fiancé, and told him to marry her even though some people would not understand what was happening.

THE FALL

Joseph listened to the angel and trusted God. He loved Mary and took care of her. **SURELY MANY PEOPLE THOUGHT THIS YOUNG COUPLE WAS VERY FOOLISH.** But Mary and Joseph trusted God and believed His promises. So, there they were, in the little town of Nazareth, waiting for Jesus to be born.

When Mary was almost ready to have the baby, the king made a law that everyone had to go back to their hometowns to pay a special tax. Joseph and

Mary began the long journey to Joseph's hometown, Bethlehem. When they arrived, they must have been ready to rest, but they couldn't find anywhere to stay. All the rooms were full. Finally, someone offered them room where the animals stayed, which was probably smelly and dirty.

Very soon, it was time for Mary's baby to be born. A cry pierced the night, and the baby was born right there among the animals. Mary swaddled Him in a cloth and laid Him down gently on the hay in a feeding trough. Perhaps she looked into His eyes as she first said His name—*Jesus*.

Not far away, shepherds were watching sheep on the hillside. Suddenly singing angels filled the sky and told the shepherds to go find the baby wrapped in cloth and lying in a manger. The shepherds ran into town and saw it was true. **THERE WAS A BABY, AND THE ANGELS HAD TOLD THEM THAT HE WAS THE SAVIOR OF THE WORLD! HE WAS THE ONE WHO WOULD SAVE THEM FROM THEIR SINS AND MAKE A WAY OUT OF THE BROKENNESS.** As the shepherds marveled at the baby, Mary treasured every moment and every word in her heart.

THE VERY GOOD NEWS

Sometime later some wise men followed a star that led them straight to the house where Mary and Joseph were staying. There the wise men knelt and worshiped Jesus, offering Him precious gifts of gold, frankincense, and myrrh. Mary surely thanked the wise men for their gifts before they left to go back to their country.

Imagine young Mary picking up her son and holding Him on her lap. She must have thought back to the night in the stable when she held her baby in her arms for the first time. Tears of joy probably filled Mary's eyes. No way could she have imagined the tears of pain that would one day fill her eyes. This same Mary would see her son die on the cross. For now, He was a tiny boy, but He would grow to be a man. A man who had come for a purpose. A man who had come to set His people free from their brokenness and forgive them of their sins. A man who would never depart from God's Plan yet would die for those who did. He was Mary's Son, but more than that, He was the only Son of God. He was the way God would forgive, restore, and bless all kinds of people from all over the world. Jesus was God's Very Good News!

WHAT ARE THREE EMOTIONS YOU THINK MARY FELT FROM THE TIME THE ANGEL VISITED HER TO THE TIME JESUS WAS BORN?

15

A HOLE IN THE ROOF

MARK 2:1-12

THE PLAN

Jesus grew into a man and began to teach others about God's Plan and design. **HE BEGAN TO TELL PEOPLE WHY HE HAD COME INTO THE WORLD. HE HEALED THE SICK.** He taught people things no one had ever heard. He loved others in a most genuine way they had never felt. Crowds were often around Jesus, bringing Him sick people to heal and listening to Him teach.

One day Jesus was in a house teaching about God's love for the world He had created. As He was teaching, the house filled with people. The room was so full that people were probably stepping on each other's toes and bumping into each other with every wiggle. But still more people came, just to hear what the great teacher Jesus was saying. They crammed in the doorway and peeked in the windows. Many of them had no clue they were listening to God's Rescuer who had been promised for thousands of years. They didn't understand that Jesus was God's one and only Son!

Soon the house was so crowded that there wasn't room for anyone else to get near Jesus.

THE FALL

Four men came to the house carrying **a friend who was paralyzed and helpless**. The men saw the crowded house, but they were determined to get their friend to Jesus. They decided to somehow get their friend onto the roof of the house—yes, the roof!

There they probably had to begin chipping away at the clay and the wood that held the roof together.

The people in the house might have looked up as bits of clay and wood fell on their shoulders. Soon they could see sunlight. And then, right there, in the room where Jesus was teaching, a man was suddenly being lowered through a hole in the roof by his friends! Jesus stopped teaching and looked up at the four men. He watched as the paralyzed man was lowered to the

ground in front of Him. Seeing the faith and determination of the men on the roof, Jesus told the paralyzed man that his sins were forgiven! It was a surprising thing to say. All the people were probably expecting Jesus to say, "You're healed!"

The religious leaders in the room were watching carefully. The healing would have been fine. But the forgiveness? Jesus's claim to forgive the man's sins greatly upset them. The leaders whispered among themselves that only God could forgive sins. *Who is Jesus that He thinks He can forgive sins?* They had Jesus all wrong. He wasn't just some man—He was God's own Son who had come to heal them from the brokenness caused by their sins.

THE VERY GOOD NEWS

Jesus knew what they were thinking. He wanted to show He had the power to heal the physical as well as the spiritual brokenness. **JESUS TOLD THE PARALYZED MAN TO GET UP, TAKE HIS THINGS, AND WALK HOME.** As soon as the man heard Jesus's words, he stood up! He didn't wobble. He didn't stumble. He just picked up his mat and walked out. Everyone squished together and made a path for him. Shock and amazement filled their faces. They couldn't believe what they had just witnessed. They began to give God the glory for it all.

The man's four friends must have celebrated as they saw their friend walk home for the first time. That day, they knew something most people in that house didn't know. It wasn't about getting in the house to hear good teaching and be a part of a cool crowd of people. No, it was about getting their friend to the feet of Jesus. They knew their friend needed to meet Jesus for himself.

This is why Jesus came into the world—to deal with brokenness. He came to forgive, to heal, to restore, and to bless. Jesus knew it would cost Him everything to deal with the sins of the people in the world. He would have to experience more brokenness than anyone. He would take on everyone's brokenness so they wouldn't have to. He would provide the way for people to repent and believe. This was why He had come.

CAN YOU NAME THREE DIFFERENT EXAMPLES OF BROKENNESS? IS JESUS ABLE TO FIX EACH OF THEM?

16

The Crazy Naked Man

MARK 4:35–5:20

One evening after Jesus taught a gigantic crowd of people, He told His disciples to get their boats ready to sail across the Sea of Galilee (which is actually a really big lake, but you can see across it on a clear day). It was a calm evening, perfect for sailing. Jesus must have been tired from a day of teaching, and He fell fast asleep in the bottom of one of the boats.

Suddenly Jesus was awakened by the disciples screaming and scooping water out of the boat. A great storm had blown over them! The waves were tossing the boats, and the disciples were scared. They wanted Jesus to do something to help. Jesus stood up, looked out over the rough sea, and simply commanded everything to be still. Immediately the wind and waves stopped. Everything went back to the calm, peaceful night it had been before. Jesus asked His disciples why they were afraid. Why did they not trust in Him? But they didn't answer. The disciples only wondered who Jesus really was. **WHAT KIND OF PERSON COULD MAKE EVEN THE WIND AND WAVES DO WHAT HE SAID?** But nothing could have prepared them for what happened next.

THE PLAN

Once they reached the other side of the Sea of Galilee, Jesus had barely stepped out of the boat when a crazy, naked man ran up and fell at His feet! This man had a very sad story. **HE WAS POSSESSED BY MANY DEMONS, AND THEY CAUSED HIM TO SIN IN MANY GREAT WAYS.** Over and over again, people tried to chain him up to keep him from hurting himself and other people. But this guy would burst through the chains, and there was no way to control him. He left his family and friends to live alone, naked in the graveyard. He was always yelling and crying, and he cut himself with rocks. No one would come near him or love him; the demons were too scary. This man was unlovable and broken beyond repair. Or at least that's what everyone thought.

THE FALL

As the man ran and knelt at Jesus's feet, Jesus commanded the demons to leave the man alone. Jesus didn't run from the man. Jesus loved the unlovable. And He wasn't afraid of demons. The demons asked Jesus what He wanted them to do. They said their name was Legion because so many of them lived in the man. Those demons knew Jesus was the Son of God and the one who had come to fix the brokenness in the world. Because they knew His special power and identity, they were scared Jesus would send them far away. They begged Jesus to let them go into a herd of pigs on a hill nearby. Jesus gave them permission, and at once the demons left the crazy, naked man and entered the pigs. Then suddenly all two thousand pigs rushed over a cliff and drowned in the sea.

Some of the people ran into town and told everyone what had happened. They told about the crazy, naked man and the pigs! Everyone came running back to the shore to see for themselves. They couldn't believe what they saw. The crazy, naked man wasn't acting crazy; he was normal. The man was sitting and talking to Jesus. And he wasn't naked, he was clothed! He wasn't a crazy, naked man anymore; he was a normal, clothed man! Ordinarily this would be a good thing, but it terrified the people who saw it happen. Those people didn't understand who Jesus was, and they were afraid of His power. They all begged Jesus to get back into His boat and go away. Well, all but one. The now normal, clothed man was begging to go with Jesus. Jesus had just fixed the man's deep brokenness, and the man wanted to be with Him.

Jesus told the man He had a better Plan. He told the now normal, clothed man to go back to his family and friends and tell them all about what God had done for him. The man's story was powerful, and he needed to share it! And that's just what the now normal, clothed man did. He went back and told his family and friends all Jesus had done for him. But he didn't stop there. The man traveled all through the ten nearby cities telling his story. He told them how he was a crazy, naked man and how Jesus made him a normal, clothed man. Everyone who heard his story was amazed and wondered at who this Jesus was.

Jesus would later come back to that same shore and visit some of the areas where the now normal, clothed man had told his story. And this time the people were eager to listen to Jesus and hear about how He was able to fix their brokenness. They wanted to learn how they could recover and pursue God's Plan just like the crazy, naked man had done. Because in their own ways, they were all crazy, naked men and women who needed to be made normal, clothed men and women. **THEY KNEW JESUS WAS THE ONE WHO COULD FORGIVE THEM, RESTORE THEM, AND BLESS THEM.**

THE VERY GOOD NEWS

WHAT DO YOU
THINK YOU WOULD HAVE
DONE IF YOU HAD BEEN
THERE TO SEE JESUS CALM
THE STORM AND DRIVE OUT
THE DEMONS?

17

A DAD AND HIS TWO SONS

LUKE 15:11-32

Jesus went all over teaching and healing. When He taught, He often used parables, which were stories that those listening could understand. But these weren't just stories with no meaning. **THE PARABLES JESUS TOLD HAD A PURPOSE—THE STORIES SHOWED SOMETHING TRUE ABOUT GOD'S PLAN.** Jesus told parables about farmers and plants, treasures, workers and masters, sheep, banquets, friends and enemies, and much more. One of His parables was about a man and his two sons. It goes like this. . . .

THE PLAN

A loving dad had two sons. The sons knew that one day when their father died, they would get an inheritance. That means the boys would split everything their dad owned. The older son was a hard worker and tried to obey and honor his dad. But the younger son just wanted to go to parties and have fun. He didn't like working or listening to what his dad said. One day the younger son asked his dad for his share of his inheritance. He didn't want to wait until his dad died; he wanted everything right away. The dad agreed to the younger son's request for his share of the family money. Soon the younger son was headed out to another land where he could live by his own rules and do things his own way.

Out on his own, the younger son got to make his own rules. His dad wasn't around to tell him what to do or give him advice. His dad wasn't there to warn him about the wrong kinds of friends or to help him make wise money decisions. So . . . the son made the wrong kinds of friends. The son made foolish decisions with his money. The son partied and partied and spent and spent, and soon he was completely broke. No one wanted to hang out with him since he was out of money. No one wanted to be his friend if he couldn't afford to party. He had no one. **THE YOUNG MAN WAS SAD, ALONE, AND DESOLATE. TO PUT IT SIMPLY, HE WAS BROKEN.**

THE FALL

The son needed to make enough money to buy food, but the only job he could find was feeding pigs. Day after day he would watch the smelly, muddy pigs eat the slop he gave them. He was so hungry that the rotten, slimy, stinky, squishy, awful, just plain disgusting pig slop started to look good! The son realized that his dad's servants ate real food and not pig slop. The son knew that if he returned home, his dad would love him and forgive him and feed him. And even though he was really embarrassed, he decided to go home. The son planned to ask his dad if he could be one of his servants so at least he could eat real food made for humans. He got up, left the pig pen, and started his journey home.

As the young son got close to home, his dad saw him on the horizon and ran to meet him. The son started to explain how sorry he was about leaving his dad and wasting his money. The son knew he didn't deserve forgiveness. He planned to ask if he could just be his father's servant. Much to his amazement, his dad wasn't mad. He had been afraid his son had died, so now the dad must've hugged him so tightly the son thought his eyeballs might pop out! The dad called for a special feast to be prepared and had his finest robe placed on the son, along with new sandals and a ring. The son's return was something to celebrate!

Meanwhile, the older son was working in the field. He heard music and saw people dancing happily. A servant told him that the father was throwing a party because his youngest son had come home. The older son was mad. All this time, he had been obedient to his dad and had never wasted his money. But their father had never honored him with a party. Now when the disrespectful younger son wastes everything and comes back with nothing, he gets a huge party! *Not fair!* the older son must have thought, and he refused to join the party.

The father loved the older son too and tried to explain that his younger brother had already spent his half of the family money. From now on, all the family money belonged to the older son. But right now, they needed to celebrate because the younger brother was alive! He was lost but now was found!

The Very Good News

Jesus shared this parable because He knew some listeners were like the younger brother. They had sinned and left God's Plan. They were completely broken. **JESUS WANTED THEM TO KNOW THAT IF THEY REPENTED, GOD WOULD WELCOME THEM BACK WITH OPEN ARMS, AND THE ANGELS IN HEAVEN WOULD CELEBRATE!** But He also knew some listeners were like the older brother. They worked hard to do what they thought God wanted, but they were jealous when others came back to God after doing many bad things. These people needed to be excited when sinners repented and came back to God to recover and follow His Plan. Jesus came to offer God's forgiveness, restoration, and blessing to *all* kinds of people. He was teaching that God's love is incredible and perfect. He loves all His children, and He never gives up on them, no matter what.

ALTHOUGH THE TWO BROTHERS WERE BROKEN AND SINFUL IN DIFFERENT WAYS, WHY DID THEY NEED TO HEAR THE SAME GOOD NEWS?

18

Jesus Fixes the Brokenness

Matthew 26–28; John 19–20

It was almost time for Jesus to do what He came into the world to do. Jesus traveled with His disciples to Jerusalem to celebrate the Passover meal. The disciples didn't know, but this would be the last meal Jesus would eat with them before He died. Before they ate, Jesus washed their feet.

THE PLAN

He told them that just as He served them, they needed to serve each other. They needed to serve all people.

Once they were seated around the table, Jesus took the bread and broke it into pieces. He said the bread represented His body, which would be broken for the disciples and for all the world's people. This was a way Jesus gave His followers to remember Him. From this time on, when they ate the bread together, they should remember His broken body. Then He took the cup of wine and told the disciples it represented His blood, which would be poured out for them. From this time on, when they drank the wine together, they should remember the blood of Jesus. The disciples didn't fully understand what He meant, but soon they would.

Jesus told the disciples one of them would betray Him. Soon Judas got up and left.

After the Passover meal was finished, Jesus went to a garden to pray. It was time for Him to fix the brokenness, although He knew it would be hard and painful. Soon Judas arrived with a bunch of soldiers. He walked up to Jesus and kissed Him on the cheek. It was a betraying kiss, full of brokenness. The soldiers arrested Jesus and took Him before the religious leaders, who asked Jesus if He claimed to be the Son of God. They were so angry with Him that they wanted to kill Him.

It was now Friday morning. The religious leaders brought Jesus to the Roman ruler Pontius Pilate, who listened to their case against Jesus. He found Jesus to be guiltless. This wasn't what the religious leaders wanted to hear. The religious leaders gathered a huge crowd of people and created a big scene. **The leaders and the people demanded that Pilate crucify Jesus.** Pontius Pilate wanted this whole situation to go away, so he ordered his soldiers to give Jesus a beating.

THE FALL

Perhaps Pontius Pilate thought the beating would satisfy the anger of the religious leaders and the mob of people. But he was wrong. The people screamed louder and louder for Jesus to be crucified. Finally, Pilate washed his hands of Jesus's life and sent Him away to be crucified.

The soldiers shoved a crown of thorns on Jesus's head, gave Him a heavy cross, and made Him carry it up the hill where they would crucify Him. Jesus was too hurt and tired to make it up the hill on his own, so the soldiers grabbed a man from the crowd and made him carry Jesus's cross.

At the top of the hill, the soldiers drove nails through His hands and feet and into the wood. They lifted the cross, and there Jesus hung, nailed to the cross. At lunchtime the sky grew dark. It was a dark day indeed.

At three in the afternoon, Jesus said, "IT IS FINISHED!" He let out one last breath, dropped His head, and died. He had taken all the sins and all the brokenness of the world—every sin of every person who believed in Him, in the past and in the future. For them He had died, like a lamb who was being sacrificed. The cross is how Jesus was going to fix all the brokenness.

Jesus's body was buried in a tomb. The Romans placed a giant stone over the entrance so no one could steal His body.

Saturday was a day unlike any other. Satan thought he had won. The disciples were hiding and confused. They were scared they might be arrested and crucified next. Mary and the women wept. It was a day of waiting, but Sunday was coming.

On Sunday morning, a few of the ladies ran to anoint Jesus's body in the tomb, but when they arrived, the giant stone had been rolled away. The tomb was empty! Suddenly an angel spoke to them and told them the good news—**JESUS WAS ALIVE! HE HAD RISEN FROM THE DEAD JUST AS HE HAD SAID!**

THE VERY GOOD NEWS

Over the next forty days, Jesus visited the disciples and many others. He proved He had risen from the dead and gave them final instructions. Jesus told them He would send a helper, the Holy Spirit, and that the disciples had this important message to spread: God has a Plan, and even though everyone sins and ends up in brokenness, He loves them and wants them to be forgiven, healed, and restored. They just have to repent of their sins and believe in what Jesus did for them on the cross and that He was raised from the dead. Then they could begin to recover and pursue God's Plan! After giving them this message, Jesus went back to heaven to be with God.

WHAT DO YOU THINK IT WAS LIKE FOR JESUS TO LIVE HIS LIFE KNOWING HE HAD TO SUFFER AS A PART OF GOD'S PLAN?

19

THE TELEPORTING MAN

ACTS 8:26-40

THE PLAN

The disciples did indeed receive the Holy Spirit, and **THEY DID EXACTLY WHAT JESUS HAD TOLD THEM TO DO: TELL EVERYONE THE GOOD NEWS ABOUT JESUS.** A disciple named Philip went to a town called Samaria to preach to the people there about God's love for them. He told them how Jesus came and lived a perfect life, died for their sins, and rose from the dead. Philip cast out demons and healed many people in the name of Jesus. Many repented and believed, and great joy filled the city. But one day an angel spoke to Philip and told him to leave Samaria and go to a desert road in the middle of nowhere. Philip must have been a little confused, but he listened and immediately went to the desert road.

At that very moment, a man from Ethiopia (that's a huge country in Africa) was traveling down that same road. He was an important government official who worked for the queen and took care of her treasure. This Ethiopian man loved God and wanted to know Him. He was on his way back to Ethiopia after making the long journey to worship God in Jerusalem. While riding in his chariot, he was reading from the Old Testament. The Ethiopian man wanted to obey God, but he did not understand what he was reading.

The Holy Spirit told Philip to go and meet the Ethiopian man's chariot. So Philip took off running.

When Philip caught up to the chariot, he listened to what the Ethiopian man was reading. It was from the book of Isaiah in the Bible. Isaiah was one of the prophets who had spoken for God to the southern tribes of Judah. God's people had written down Isaiah's words and saved them for many, many years. The Ethiopian man was reading the part where Isaiah wrote about Jesus the coming Savior and what would happen to Him. **THE ETHIOPIAN MAN WAS CONFUSED AND DIDN'T UNDERSTAND WHAT HE WAS READING.**

THE FALL

Philip asked the man if he knew what he was reading. The Ethiopian might have been surprised by the question, but he stopped the chariot for a conversation. Philip probably bent over to catch his breath after all that running. The man asked Philip how he could understand what he was reading if someone didn't explain it to him. Philip said he could explain. The Ethiopian invited Philip to sit with him in his chariot, and Philip gladly accepted.

Together Philip and the man read the confusing Bible verses that talked about a man who would be led to slaughter like a sheep. It said the man didn't make a sound even though He was humiliated. The Ethiopian asked if Isaiah was talking about himself or someone else. Philip probably just smiled. He must have realized why God told him to come to this desert road in the middle of nowhere. Then Philip had a gospel conversation with the Ethiopian and told him all about God's Plan and the good news about Jesus. He most likely spoke about how everyone sins and ends up in brokenness. He explained how people from the beginning of time have fallen and failed, until Jesus arrived. Philip explained who Jesus was and how He loved like no one else. He told the Ethiopian man that Jesus loved him so much that He died on the cross, a death He didn't deserve, and then rose from the dead! *That's* what the confusing verses were talking about!

THE VERY GOOD NEWS

The Ethiopian man must have listened very carefully. He took in every one of Philip's words. **PHILIP EXPLAINED THAT IF THE MAN REPENTED OF HIS SINS AND BELIEVED IN WHAT JESUS HAD DONE, HE COULD BEGIN TO RECOVER AND PURSUE GOD'S PLAN FOR HIS LIFE.** The Ethiopian must have repented and believed because right then he looked over and saw a pool of water. He asked Philip if there was anything stopping him from being baptized. Philip said nothing was stopping him! So they stopped the chariot and went down in the water, where Philip baptized him.

As soon as they came out of the water, the Holy Spirit whisked Philip away. To the Ethiopian, it must have seemed as if Philip had vanished or teleported! The man headed on his way, celebrating all that had happened to him on that special day.

Meanwhile, the Holy Spirit took Philip away to another city. He was probably a little surprised about what had just happened, but he began to preach the good news anyway. Philip had definitely obeyed Jesus's command to go and tell others about Him.

The Ethiopian rejoiced to learn the good news. How can you celebrate the good news today?

20

FROM KILLER TO TEACHER

ACTS 8–28

Not everyone was happy to hear the good news about what Jesus did on the cross. Many people wanted to imprison or even kill those who believed in Jesus. No one wanted this more than a man named Saul. Saul was a Pharisee who did not believe that Jesus was the Son of God and rose from the dead. One day Saul heard a man named Stephen preaching the good news of Jesus. The religious leaders became very angry with Stephen and decided to stone him to death. Saul approved, and Stephen was killed. Stephen was the first person to die for preaching about Jesus. This sparked a great persecution in the land. Christians were scattered everywhere, fearing for their lives.

Saul continued to persecute Christians and went house to house looking for anyone who believed in Jesus. The government gave him authority to throw Christians in jail or have them killed. Then one day, everything changed for Saul. While traveling near the city of Damascus, a bright light engulfed him and knocked him to the ground. Saul couldn't see a thing—he was blind! Fortunately, his ears were okay, and he heard a voice from heaven asking why he was doing these awful things to followers of Jesus. Saul asked, "Who are you?" The voice answered and said, "I AM Jesus."

THE PLAN **HE TOLD SAUL TO GO INTO THE CITY, WHERE HE WOULD RECEIVE MORE INSTRUCTIONS.**

The men with Saul were shocked and confused, especially when they realized that Saul couldn't see. Saul realized that Jesus really was who He said He was. Saul repented and believed in Jesus. Right then he began to learn and pursue God's Plan. He found some Christians in Damascus. A Christian named Ananias prayed for Saul, and God gave him his sight back. Ananias baptized Saul, and the Christians in Damascus (who Saul used to hate) became Saul's friends (who he learned to love). Saul was learning how Jesus changes everything.

As soon as Saul became a believer in Jesus, God called him to preach. Saul preached near and far, across the land. Soon people began to call him Paul. Paul said that he was the worst sinner who had ever lived. He said that if he could be saved by Jesus, then anyone could be saved by Jesus. He traveled with a group of people, and together they started churches all over the region. He taught men and women to lead and serve those churches. Silas, Barnabas, Timothy, Lydia, Priscilla, and Aquila—they all helped Paul start new churches. Everywhere Paul went, he tried to tell people about the good news in a way they could understand it best. Even though he was trying to point others to Jesus, not everyone wanted to hear about Him. **SOME PEOPLE WANTED PAUL IN PRISON, OR EVEN DEAD!**

THE FALL

Once when Paul was in jail for teaching the good news, God caused an earthquake, and the jail doors broke open. Paul could have easily escaped, but instead he stayed and told the jailers about Jesus. Another time Paul was being brought to a new city by boat when a storm caused the boat to sink. Paul had to swim in freezing cold water to make it to an island. Instead of trying to get back home, he stayed to tell the people on the island about Jesus! That was just how Paul was. He was always telling people about Jesus, no matter what happened or where he was or who was there.

Many times, Paul was beaten up when he tried to talk about Jesus. One time he was beaten so badly he almost died. He was thrown in prison at least four times for preaching the good news of Jesus. He was shipwrecked at least three times. He was tortured and run out of town. Yet through it all, he never stopped preaching about how Jesus was crucified for the sins of the world and raised from the dead.

Before Paul became a Christian, he spent many years training to be a Pharisee. In "Pharisee school," he had studied the Old Testament and read it many times. But after Paul became a believer in Jesus, he went back and studied the Old Testament all over again and could see that it all pointed toward the coming of Jesus. The Old Testament is full of great stories that make up the big story about God's Plan. Paul wanted to make sure followers of Jesus understood that the whole Bible is all about Jesus.

Paul knew that new believers in these new churches needed encouragement. He wrote letters to the churches, and they were passed from church to church so that everyone could understand God's Plan. He explained the importance of believing the good news and loving one another the way Jesus loved. He told them how to live as a family by making Jesus the center of their lives. As time went on, Paul's letters would make up one-third of the New Testament!

THE VERY GOOD NEWS

PAUL'S LIFE WENT FROM COMPLETE BROKENNESS TO A LIFE SPENT DISCOVERING AND PURSUING GOD'S PLAN. He understood what Jesus had done on the cross, and he wanted everyone else to understand it too. No matter the trials, challenges, or troubles he faced, Paul continued to share the good news of Jesus. He never lost sight of what Jesus had done for him. He just wanted to help others see it too.

21

YOUR STORY

Wow, what a story! These aren't all the stories in the BIG story of the Bible. They do show us the pattern that is repeated over and over again. Wouldn't it be cool if you could be in one of them? Well, your story may never be in the Bible, but it could be like them. Do you want to know how?

God has a Plan for how you should live your life. A perfect Plan. It would make God happy if you chose to follow His Plan, and it would make you super happy too. But the truth is that you don't always follow God's Plan; just like Adam and Eve, you fall too. You sin. A sin is when you do not follow God's Plan, such as when you lie, disobey your parents, or say unkind things to a friend. You think and do all sorts of things that are not part of God's Plan for you.

When we do these things, they lead to the same brokenness everyone in the Bible experienced. We feel broken because our sins separate us from God. When we sin, we owe God a debt that has to be paid somehow. We deserve to be punished for our sins. We feel broken because we have no way to pay that debt to God.

Everyone in the whole world has experienced the same kind of brokenness. Your brokenness may look different from other people's brokenness, but broken is broken. Like the people in the Bible, you try to fix it yourself, but nothing ever seems to work. Being kind seems to work for a little while, but then you are mean again. Or you tell your parents you're sorry and promise never to disobey again, but then you lie to them and find yourself in more brokenness.

How can you pay your debt to God? How will you be close to God? How will your brokenness be healed?

There is Very Good News for you . . . for all of us! When Jesus lived on earth, He followed God's Plan every single day of His life. And then Jesus died on the cross for your sins. He never sinned, and yet He took the punishment for all the things you've done and all the things you've thought about doing. He paid your debt for you. He was broken, so you don't have to stay in brokenness. This is the Very Good News!